A Note to Parents a

Dorling Kindersley Readers is a co..
programme for children, designed in conjunction with
leading literacy experts, including Cliff Moon M.Ed.,
Honorary Fellow of the University of Reading. Cliff Moon
has spent many years as a teacher and teacher educator
specializing in reading and has written more than
140 books for children and teachers. He reviews
regularly for teachers' journals.

Beautiful illustrations and superb full-colour
photographs combine with engaging, easy-to-read stories
to offer a fresh approach to each subject in the series.
Each *Dorling Kindersley Reader* is guaranteed to capture
a child's interest while developing his or her reading
skills, general knowledge, and love of reading.

The four levels of *Dorling Kindersley Readers* are
aimed at different reading abilities, enabling you to
choose the books that are exactly right for each child:

Level 1 – Beginning to read
Level 2 – Beginning to read alone
Level 3 – Reading alone
Level 4 – Proficient readers

The "normal" age at which a child begins
to read can be anywhere from three to
eight years old, so these levels are only a
general guideline. No matter which
level you select, you can be sure
that you are helping your
child learn to read,
then read to learn!

LONDON, NEW YORK, DELHI, PARIS,
MUNICH and MELBOURNE

Art Editor Jane Horne
Senior Art Editor Cheryl Telfer
Series Editor Deborah Lock
Editor Anna Lofthouse
DTP Designer Almudena Diaz
Production Shivani Pandey
Picture Researcher Jo Haddon
DK Picture Researcher Sally Hamilton
Jacket Designer Chris Drew
Illustrator Paul Weston
Indexer Lynn Bresler

Reading Consultant
Cliff Moon M.Ed.

Whale Consultant
William Rossiter, Cetacean Society International

Published in Great Britain by Dorling Kindersley Limited
80 The Strand, London, WC2R 0RL
A Penguin Company

2 4 6 8 10 9 7 5 3 1

A CIP catalogue record for this book is available
from the British Library.

ISBN 0-7513-4597-0

Colour reproduction by Colourscan, Singapore
Printed and bound in China by L Rex Printing Co., Ltd.

The publisher would like to thank the following for their kind permission to
reproduce their images:
c=centre, a=above, b=below, l=left, r=right.
Cetacean Society International: William Rossiter 2tc, 2ca, 5clb, 14-15,
16ca, 16bc, 17, 18br, 24, 25blr, 29; **J Michael Williamson Photo/Whalenet
(www.whale.wheelock.edu)**: 5crb, 7br, 26-27;
Bryan and Cherry Alexander Photography: B&C Alexander 21;
Bruce Coleman Ltd: Jim Watt 9, 12, 33br; Pacific Stock front cover, 4tc,
10tc; **Corbis**: Peter Johnson 27tr; **Environmental Images**: Roger Grace
21tr; **FLPA - Images of Nature**: Brake/Sunset 6-7; F Nicklin/Minden
Pictures 15tr; R Pitman/Earthviews 32cla; **Salvatore Siciliano**: Salvatore
Siciliano 22-23; **Still Pictures**: Ray Pfortner 32cr; **Corbis Stock Market**:
Craig Tuttle 10br; Amos Nachoum 19; **Telegraph Colour Library**:
Peter Scoones 2bc, 30-31.
All other images © Dorling Kindersley. .
For further information see: www. dkimages.com

see our complete catalogue at

DK **DORLING KINDERSLEY READERS**

Journey of a Humpback Whale

Written by Caryn Jenner

A Dorling Kindersley Book

SPLASH!

A humpback whale jumps
out of the sea.
He is called Triton (TRY-tun)
after a sea god in ancient myths.

4

Triton has a very powerful tail.
The fins at the end of his tail
are called "flukes".
Triton has special markings
under his flukes.
Every humpback whale
has different markings.
Do the flukes of these humpbacks
look different to you?

Triton's flukes

Whales live in the sea,
but they are mammals, not fish.
Triton breathes air like humans
and other mammals.
He can hold his breath under water
for about 30 minutes but
usually he swims to the surface
every 4 to 10 minutes.

Then Triton breathes through
the blow-holes on top of his head and
sprays a cloud of mist into the sky!

Blow-holes

Humpback whales
have two blow-holes.
The mist from a whale
is like your misty
breath in cold weather.

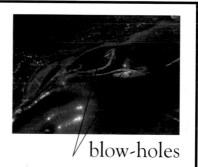

blow-holes

Sometimes Triton makes
special noises under the water.
GROAN–GRUNT–CHIRP!
Triton sings loudly and
repeats the same song
over and over again.
The eerie sounds of his song
can be heard far away.
Only male humpback whales
like Triton sing this special song.
He sings so that other whales
will know where he is,
especially female whales.

GROOOAAN GRUNT CHIRP

Triton has spent all winter
in the warm water
of the Caribbean Sea.
Now he is hungry but
there isn't much food
for a whale in the Caribbean.

Warm water
In winter, whales
swim to warm
water to mate
and to give birth
to their young.

It is time for Triton to swim
thousands of kilometres to the
far north of the Atlantic Ocean.
He lives there for most of the year.
The water is cold in the north and
Triton knows that it will be
full of good food to eat.

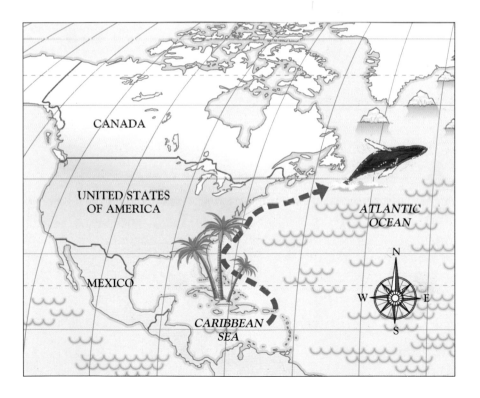

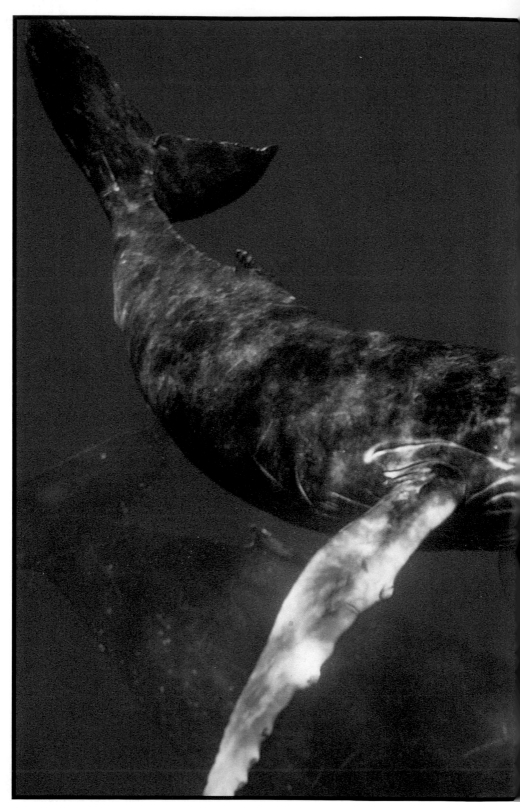

SWISH, SWISH!

Triton moves his mighty tail
up and down as he swims.
He uses his long flippers to steer.
His skin is smooth and sleek so that
he can glide through the water.

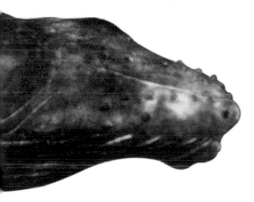

Triton swims at a
slow, steady pace.
He has a long
way to go.

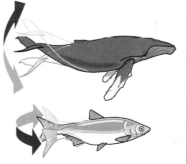

Swimming
Whales, dolphins and
porpoises move their tails
up and down to swim.
But fish move their tails
from side to side.

Triton meets his friend, Spoon,
as he swims north.
They travel together for a while,
playing as they swim.
Triton and Spoon poke their heads
out of the water and look around.

Eyes underwater

A whale's eyes are protected from the sting of the salty sea water by a clear layer of film, which covers its eyeballs.

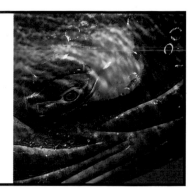

Triton listens carefully.
He can hear many sounds
that help him to know
what is in the ocean around him.
Now he hears a loud SPLASH!
What can it be?

It is Spoon.

She leaps out of the water
in a move called a "breach".

Now it's Triton's turn.

He dives backwards with his flippers
high in the air.

SPLASH!

After all that swimming and playing,
Triton and Spoon take a rest.
But Triton is only half asleep.

Part of his brain must stay awake to
remind him to swim to the surface
to take a breath of air.

A mother whale called Salt
swims nearby with her calf.
This is the calf's first journey north.
She learns to swim and dive
by watching her mother.
As she grows, the calf will develop
a layer of fat called "blubber,"
which will give her energy
when food is hard to find.
Blubber will also keep her warm
in cold water.

First breath

Sometimes, a mother whale helps her calf to the surface to take its first breath of air.

Triton dives under the water,

and swims north.

Look out!

But it's too late.

Triton gets caught in a fishing net.

He rolls around and around,

trying to escape.

He has been underwater for too long.

He must swim to the surface

to breathe.

SWISH goes his mighty tail. SWISH!

Finally, Triton finds an opening

in the net and swims through

to the surface of the water.

At last, he opens his blow-holes

and breathes the air.

Dangerous nets

Many whales and dolphins die when they are accidentally caught in nets or other fishing gear.

Triton feels weak, too weak to swim.
He drifts with the ocean tide and
it carries him to the shore.
Triton can feel the sandy seabed
scrape against the skin on his belly.
He must swim back to deep water,
or he'll be stranded
on the beach.

He tries to swish his tail.
Bit by bit, he moves backwards,
away from the shore.
His strength is coming back.
SWISH. SWISH. SWISH!

As he swims north again,
Triton hears the sound of a boat
in the distance.
It is a whale-watching boat.
The people on the boat
gaze at him in wonder.
This makes Triton feel much better.
He knows they won't hurt him.
Triton swims towards the boat.
He breaches and flicks his tail.
The people laugh and take pictures.

Whale-watching
Whale-watching boats leave from many coastal places, depending on the season.

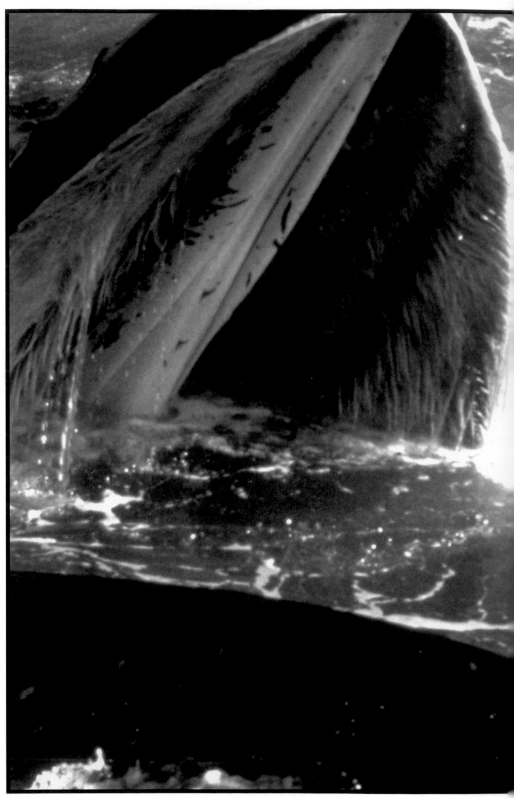

Food for whales

Humpback whales feed on small fish such as sardines, herring and tiny shrimp-like creatures called "krill".

Triton swims farther north,

where the water is colder.

He takes a giant gulp of cold water.

It is filled with many small fish.

Instead of teeth, Triton has

long bristles called "baleen".

He filters out the extra water

through his baleen,

then swallows the fish.

Delicious!

Whales gather wherever
there is enough food.
Soon Triton sees his friend, Spoon.
Together, they dive under the water,
blowing bubbles in a big circle
to catch a school of herring.
Triton surfaces,
his mouth full of fish.
SKREEK! SKREEK!
Hungry seagulls arrive to see if
Triton will share his catch.
He lets them have a few fish.
Triton is almost home,
where there will be
plenty of food for him and
for many other whales, too.

At last, Triton arrives home!
It has taken him 35 days
to swim about 3,000 kilometres
from the Caribbean Sea
to the cold waters
off the coast of Canada.

Now Triton will stay here,
swimming and playing,
and eating as much fish
as he likes.
Then, when winter comes again,
he will make the long journey south.

SAVE THE WHALES

Humpbacks like Triton are only one kind of whale. There are other kinds of whales, too, like the giant blue whale, and the square-headed sperm whale. They all need our help to survive.

Many whales have been killed by hunters on whaling ships. Whaling is now against the law in most of the world, but whales are still in danger.

Fishing equipment, such as nets and traps, is one of the main dangers to whales and dolphins. Luckily, Triton escaped from the fishing net, but it left scars on his skin.

Pollution is extremely harmful to whales. Imagine gulping down a mouthful of chemicals and other rubbish along with your fish. It could be deadly.

Help to protect whales and other sea creatures by cleaning litter off the beaches. Cleaner beaches make for cleaner oceans.

To find out about whales, how to help them, and where to go whale-watching, contact:

Whale and Dolphin Conservation Society, Alexander House, James St West, Bath, BA1 2BT, United Kingdom (www.wdcs.org)

To find out more about saving the Earth's natural resources, including whales and other animals contact:

Greenpeace International, Keizersgracht 176, 1016 DW Amsterdam, The Netherlands (www.greenpeace.org)